Understanding
the Human Body

Understanding
Food and Digestion

Robert Snedden

rosen publishing's
rosen
central

New York

Published in 2010 by The Rosen Publishing Group Inc.
29 East 21st Street, New York, NY 10010

First Edition

Library of Congress Cataloging-in-Publication Data

Snedden, Robert.
  Understanding food and digestion / Robert Snedden. -- 1st ed.
      p. cm. -- (Understanding the human body)
  Includes index.
  ISBN 978-1-4358-9687-1 (library binding)
  ISBN 978-1-4358-9693-2 (paperback)
  ISBN 978-1-4358-9694-9 (6-pack)
  1. Digestion--Juvenile literature. 2. Gastrointestinal system--Juvenile literature. I. Title.
  QP145.S574 2010
  612.3--dc22
                              2009028026

Photo Credits:
Getty Images: p. 11 (National Geographic), p. 27 (Dr. David M. Phillips), p. 30 (Dr. Kessel & Dr. Kardon/Tissues & Organs); istockphoto.com: cover (Chris Bernard), p. 6 (RonTech2000), p. 8 (heidijdesign), title page and p. 9 (HSNPhotography), p. 37 (Nathan Watkins); NASA: p. 21; Science Photo Library: p. 12 (Clive Freeman, The Royal Institution), p. 14 (OMIKRON), p. 23 (Eye of Science), p. 34 (Biomedical Imaging Unit, Southampton General Hospital); Shutterstock Images: p. 17 (Nemanja Glumac), p. 19 (Gelpi), pp. 25, 35 (Filipe B. Varela), p. 29 (Brasiliao-media), p. 31 (Factoria singular fotografia), p. 32 (PHOTO 888), p. 36 (Alfred Wekelo), p. 38 (Robert Gubbins), p. 39 (Floris Slooff), p. 40 (kristian sekulic), p. 41 (Richard Fitzer), p. 42 (ahnhuynh), p. 43 (Victoria German)

Manufactured in China
CPSIA Compliance Information: Batch #WAW0102YA: For Further Information contact
Rosen Publishing, New York, New York at 1-800-237-9932

Contents

Eat to live

Why do we need to eat? We eat because the human body needs a constant supply of energy and raw materials. It needs energy to keep functioning, to send impulses through the nervous system, to keep the heart beating, and to make other movements. It needs materials to carry out repairs and to grow. The source of both the energy and the materials that our bodies need is the food we eat.

The digestive system

The body can't use the energy and raw materials from food directly. First, the food has to be digested. This is a process that makes the nutrients in the food available.

The process of digestion begins in the mouth when we first take a bite of food and begin to chew it. This is the first stage in breaking down food into tiny fragments that the body's cells can use. Once you swallow it, the food disappears from sight and your hunger is satisfied.

Most of the digestive process takes place automatically without any need for conscious thought from us. It continues in the stomach where the food is churned with strong acids. The food becomes a semidigested mush and

A good meal provides our bodies with the energy and raw materials it needs.

passes into the intestines. Here, additional digestion takes place and the nutrients released are taken up into the bloodstream.

We don't get consciously involved in the digestion process again until we feel the need to go to the bathroom. This is when we get rid of the indigestible leftovers of the food we ate.

Cell power

Every part of your body, including the digestive system, is made up of microscopically small living cells. Each one is like a tiny chemical factory where thousands of reactions take place every second. Different substances are continually being broken down, reassembled, and combined with other substances to make new ones. Some reactions release energy, others use energy. The total of all the reactions going on in the body at any one time is called metabolism.

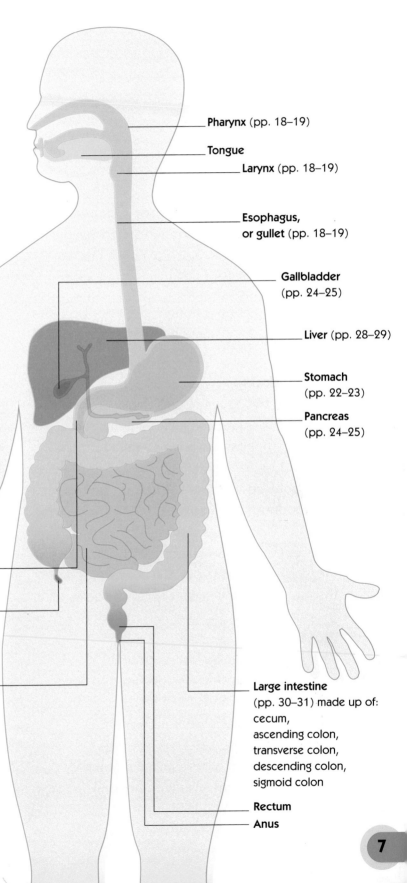

Pharynx (pp. 18–19)

Tongue

Larynx (pp. 18–19)

Esophagus, or gullet (pp. 18–19)

Gallbladder (pp. 24–25)

Liver (pp. 28–29)

Stomach (pp. 22–23)

Pancreas (pp. 24–25)

Duodenum
first part of small intestine

Appendix
(p. 31)

Small intestine
(pp. 26–27)

Large intestine
(pp. 30–31) made up of:
cecum,
ascending colon,
transverse colon,
descending colon,
sigmoid colon

Rectum

Anus

▶ The human digestive system includes the esophagus, liver, stomach, pancreas, and intestines.

What's on your plate?

Plants can capture the energy of sunlight. They can make new plant material from carbon dioxide in the air and water and minerals from the soil. Humans can't do this. The food we eat has to supply all of the body's needs for energy, maintenance, and growth. So what are the basic components in food that the body needs to stay healthy?

Food groups

The food we eat contains many different things, but much of it can be divided into three main groups: carbohydrates, proteins, and fats. Some foods will be made up almost entirely of one of these foodstuffs, but others will be a mixture. In addition to the three main groups, the body also needs tiny amounts of vitamins and minerals.

Carbohydrates

There are two types of carbohydrate: simple carbohydrates and complex carbohydrates. Simple carbohydrates are also called simple sugars. They are found in foods such as table sugar, confectionery, milk, and fruit. Complex carbohydrates, such as starch, are basically long chains of sugar molecules joined together. Sources of complex carbohydrates include bread, rice, and potatoes. Carbohydrates are the fuel that supplies the energy the cells need.

Proteins

Your body uses proteins for all kinds of essential activities. Proteins are used to build and maintain the body. They are part of your body's defenses against disease and they speed up chemical reactions (see page 12). Also, it is a type of protein in red blood cells that carries oxygen around the body. This protein is called hemoglobin.

The body cannot use proteins in food directly. First they have to be broken down into smaller units called amino acids, as part of the digestive process. Then the amino acids have to be reassembled into more proteins. Meat, fish, eggs, beans, and cheese are all sources of proteins.

Foods such as whole-wheat bread and pasta are very high in energy-giving carbohydrates.

Fish is a good source of the proteins that we need for many essential bodily functions.

Fats

The body uses some of the components of fats in building cells. Fats also cushion and protect many organs and insulate the body from cold. Like carbohydrates, they provide the body with energy. Cheese, meats, and oils, such as sunflower oil, are all sources of fat.

Vitamins and minerals

These are chemicals that the body needs in small amounts to allow its cells to work properly. For instance, the mineral calcium is essential for bone-building. Some vitamins are involved in the building of larger molecules and in chemical reactions in cells. The body can't make vitamins itself, but you can get all of the vitamins and minerals you need from a healthy, balanced diet.

Investigate

Many people today want to know what is in the foods they buy, and there are rules about the labeling of food. All the ingredients in a food product have to be listed on the packaging together with how much of each ingredient the food contains. Next time you visit the supermarket, take a look at the food labels. Find out which foods have high salt and sugar contents. It is important to be aware of this, since too much salt and sugar in the diet is known to cause health problems.

A balanced diet

We need a mixture of foodstuffs to stay healthy, but what sort of proportions should we be eating them in? For instance, it wouldn't be very healthy to be eating mainly carbohydrates and only a little protein. For good health, our diet has to be balanced and contain the right amounts from each food group.

What is a diet?

To many people the word "diet" might mean some kind of weight loss program, but "diet" also means the food that you eat regularly. The more balanced your diet and the more nutritious the items in it, the healthier you will be.

Age and change

At different stages in our lives, we may need different things from our diet. Young children are growing and developing very rapidly. Because of this, they need a diet that is high in energy and nutrients.

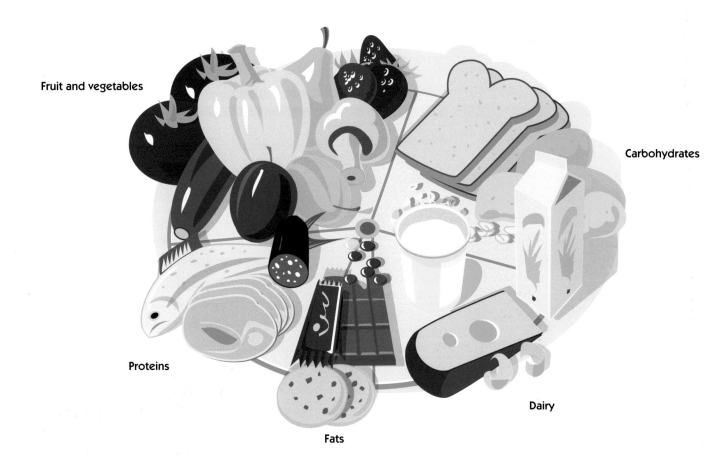

Fruit and vegetables

Carbohydrates

Proteins

Fats

Dairy

▲ A balanced diet will include many different types of food to ensure that the body gets all it needs to stay healthy.

Older people can benefit from a diet that is high in fiber. The digestive system gets less efficient at moving food along as age increases, and fiber assists the passage of food through the intestines. Older people also need a diet that is rich in the mineral iron, since the body's ability to absorb this decreases with age.

Diet and weight

What food you eat will affect what you weigh. Recent research into children's eating habits has confirmed that a diet that is high in fat and low in fiber causes children to become fat. The researchers found that a child with a diet rich in white bread, potato chips, cookies, and processed meats was four times more likely to gain weight as body fat than a child whose diet included fresh fruit and vegetables, high-fiber breakfast cereals, and whole-grain breads.

Inuit diet

A healthy, balanced diet can take different forms, some of which are not obviously healthy at first sight.

The traditional diet of the Inuit who live in the Arctic is an unusual one. It consists mainly of seal meat, fat, and blubber (the thick layer of fat found in animals such as seals and whales). The Inuit diet contains very little fresh fruit or any other type of plant material. The Inuit people stay healthy because the foods they eat are not only high in protein and energy content, but also rich in a number of essential vitamins. These include vitamin C, E, A, and D. Inuit people probably get more vitamin C from their diet than we do.

Investigate

Do you know how well-balanced your diet is? Try keeping a food diary for a week. Write down everything you eat and try not to cheat by forgetting a chocolate-chip cookie or two! Then, at the end of the week, make a chart showing how much of each food you've been eating. Will the results be what you expect?

These Inuit children stay healthy on a diet that includes things such as muktuk—boiled whale skin and blubber.

Essential enzymes

The human body relies on a huge number of chemical reactions. Some of the most important of these reactions take place when we digest our food. These reactions are controlled by means of special types of molecules called enzymes.

Catalysts and enzymes

Catalysts are substances that can make chemical reactions go faster without themselves being changed by the reaction. This allows a catalyst to be used over and over again. Enzymes are catalysts that are made by living things.

All enzymes are proteins and work best when conditions are right for them. Most enzymes will quickly stop working if the temperature is too high. Although enzymes in the stomach need acid conditions to be effective, others in the small intestine are prevented from working by acidity.

Many enzymes are involved in breaking down large food molecules during the process of digestion. For example, the enzyme amylase is present in saliva. Once you have swallowed the food, the amylase stops working. This is because of the acid in the stomach.

Substrates

Enzymes are very specific in what they do—each one will only be involved with one particular reaction. Digestive enzymes break large food molecules up into smaller ones, but other enzymes assemble big molecules from small ones. The substance that the enzyme works on is called the substrate.

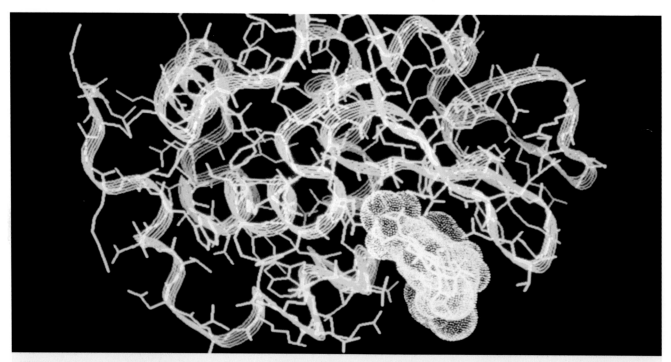

This computer generated image shows how a substrate (yellow) fits into the complex folds of an enzyme (purple) like a key fitting inside a lock.

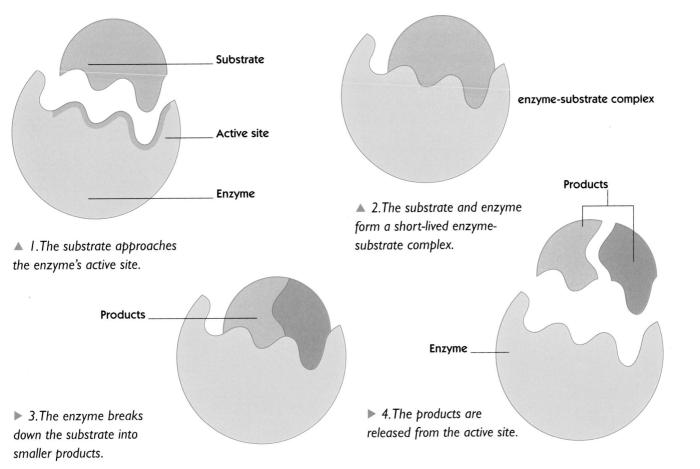

▲ 1. The substrate approaches the enzyme's active site.

▲ 2. The substrate and enzyme form a short-lived enzyme-substrate complex.

▶ 3. The enzyme breaks down the substrate into smaller products.

▶ 4. The products are released from the active site.

Lock and key

An enzyme reaction can be broken down into four stages.

1) The enzyme and the substrate have to be brought into contact with each other.

2) The substrate links up with the enzyme at an area on the enzyme called the active site. The active site is shaped so that only one particular molecule will fit into it. It is like a lock that only one key will fit. For example, if the temperature is too high or conditions are too acidic, the enzyme loses its shape.

The substrate "key" will no longer fit the enzyme "lock."

3) While it is "locked in" to the enzyme, the substrate is changed by a chemical reaction. For example, starch becomes sugar. The new substances formed by this reaction are called the products.

4) Because the products are a different shape from the substrate, they no longer fit the enzyme lock and are released. The enzyme is ready for another substrate molecule and the process can start again.

Tasting and chewing

We begin the process of digestion by biting and chewing our food. But other important things also happen to food inside your mouth. The tongue tastes the food, giving us a lot of pleasure when the food is tasty. Food that is unsafe to eat sometimes tastes unpleasant, providing a warning that the food may be bad.

Taste buds

We all have things that we like to eat more than others, and largely that is down to taste. We may also come to dislike foods that we associate with being sick. Even if it wasn't the food itself that made us sick, the memory of the illness can cause us to find its taste unappealing.

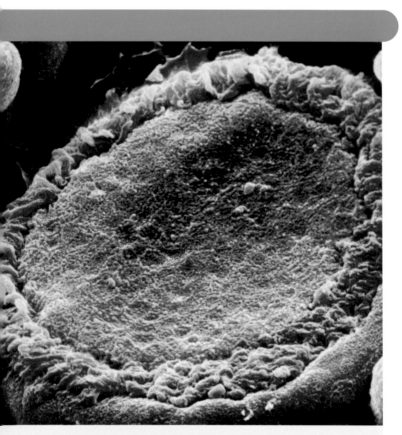

This is what a group of taste buds looks like under the microscope.

The sense of taste begins with clusters of specialized cells called taste buds, found on the surface of the tongue. The little bumps that you can see on your tongue are not taste buds—taste buds are too small to see without a microscope. But these bumps, called papillae, are where most taste buds are found.

The taste buds detect the flavor molecules in what we eat and pass this information on to the brain via the taste nerves. This triggers other activities, such as increasing the production of saliva and preparing the stomach to receive the food.

Taste types

Humans recognize five basic flavors:

- **Sweet** usually a sign that food is energy-rich

- **Salty** salts are essential for normal body functions

- **Bitter** sometimes a sign that the food may be bad, or rotten

- **Sour** often the sign of acidity in food

- **Umami** (**meaty flavor**) detected in protein-rich foods.

▶ *Three main pairs of salivary glands produce saliva and secrete it into the mouth. These glands are located below the ear, under the lower jaw bone, and under the tongue.*

Salivary gland

Tongue

Salivary glands

Salivary glands

Three pairs of salivary glands positioned around the mouth produce saliva, making the food moist and easier to chew and swallow. Saliva does a number of important things.

- The mucus in saliva is very good at binding chewed up food fragments into a slippery mass called a bolus. This can slide easily through the gullet (see page 7) to the stomach.

- It coats the inside of the mouth and gullet. This helps to protect the cells of the mouth and gullet tissues.

- It dissolves dry food—if this didn't happen, we wouldn't taste it.

- It flushes out the mouth, helping to remove food remains and keeping the mouth clean.

- It contains lysozyme, an enzyme that kills many bacteria.

- It contains amylase, an enzyme that begins to digest starch into maltose (a type of sugar).

Body facts

The inside of your mouth is warm and humid, just like conditions in a rainforest. These conditions, together with a regular supply of food coming in, make it an ideal place for bacteria and other microorganisms to flourish. There are hundreds of different kinds of these tiny living things making their homes between your teeth, on the roof of your mouth, and on your tongue. The total of the organisms in your mouth outnumber the people in the world.

Take a bite

The first thing we have to do to start the process of digestion is to get the food into our mouths. With most foods, this means we have to take a bite, using our teeth to break the food up into smaller pieces. In this form, the food is more easily swallowed and digested.

Teeth for tasks

Although some people may choose to have a vegetarian diet, humans evolved as omnivores—eating both animal and vegetable matter. This fact is reflected in the teeth we have, which are a cross between those found in carnivores (flesh-eaters, such as dogs) and herbivores (plant-eaters, such as horses). Adult humans have four different kinds of teeth and a total of 32 teeth.

At the front of the mouth are the sharp-edged incisors, which are used to cut and bite our food. We have a total of eight incisors, four in the top jaw and four in the bottom.

▶ This cross section diagram shows the structure of a tooth, together with the blood vessels and nerves that extend into the pulp cavity at the centre of the tooth.

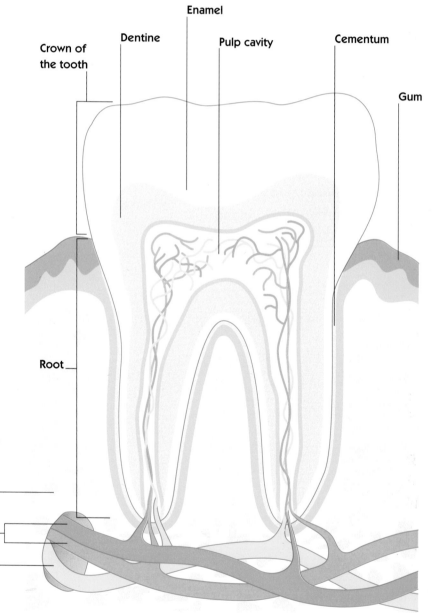

Enamel

Dentine

Pulp cavity

Cementum

Crown of the tooth

Gum

Root

Bone

Blood vessels

Nerve

Next to the incisors are the pointed canines, which are used for gripping and tearing food. Carnivores have canines, but herbivores do not. We have four of these canines, two in each jaw.

Just behind the canines are the premolars. These teeth are located between the canines and the flatter molars at the back of the mouth. They are broader than the canines, but smaller than the molars. They can chop and grind the food. We have eight premolars.

At the back of the mouth are the flat-topped molars. These are used to grind and crush the food into a pulp for swallowing. Carnivores do not have molars, but herbivores do. We have 12 molars.

Tooth anatomy

The crown of the tooth is the part extending above the gum. It is encased in enamel, the hardest substance in the body. Beneath the enamel is dentine, a bonelike material that makes up the bulk of the tooth. Within the dentine is the pulp cavity. The pulp cavity holds blood vessels and nerves. The root of the tooth is held in place in the jaw by a type of calcium-rich connective tissue called cementum.

Tooth decay

Tooth decay is caused by the buildup of plaque on the teeth. This is a sticky deposit made up of food remains, saliva, and bacteria. Left alone, it will harden into tartar. Tartar and plaque produce acids, which can gradually dissolve the tooth enamel and create cavities. If a cavity grows large enough to expose the pulp

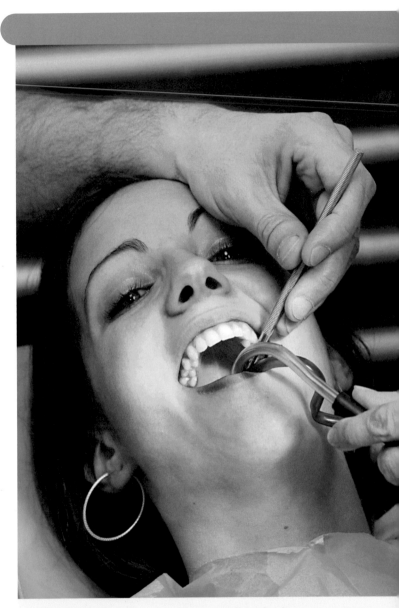

It is important to take care of your teeth; a checkup at the dentist every six months can help prevent the problems that lead to toothache and tooth loss.

inside the tooth, the result is a painful toothache. Regular brushing is essential to get rid of plaque, and it is also a good idea to rinse your mouth after eating sticky foods.

Swallowing

Once the food in your mouth has been chewed and savored, it is time to send it on its way to the stomach for the next stage in digestion. Swallowing a mouthful of food might seem like a very simple act, but it is a much more complex process than it appears to be.

Forming a bolus

First the tongue shapes the food into a ball, called a bolus, and propels it to the back of the mouth. The roof of the mouth is called the palate. It is hard at the front but soft toward the back. If you press your tongue against your palate, you should be able to feel the difference.

As the tongue moves the bolus of food toward the back of the mouth, it is pressed into the pharynx. The pharynx is the back of the throat, leading to the esophagus, or gullet. This movement with the tongue is the only part of the swallowing process that is voluntary. Beyond this step, everything happens by reflex, or without your conscious control.

▼ *The food bolus is in the mouth.*

▼ *The food bolus enters the throat. The soft palate moves upward to stop food from entering the nasal cavity. The larynx moves forward and the epiglottis closes over it to stop food from going down the windpipe.*

▼ *The food bolus is going down the esophagus. The epiglottis, larynx, and soft palate are back in the same position as in fig. 1.*

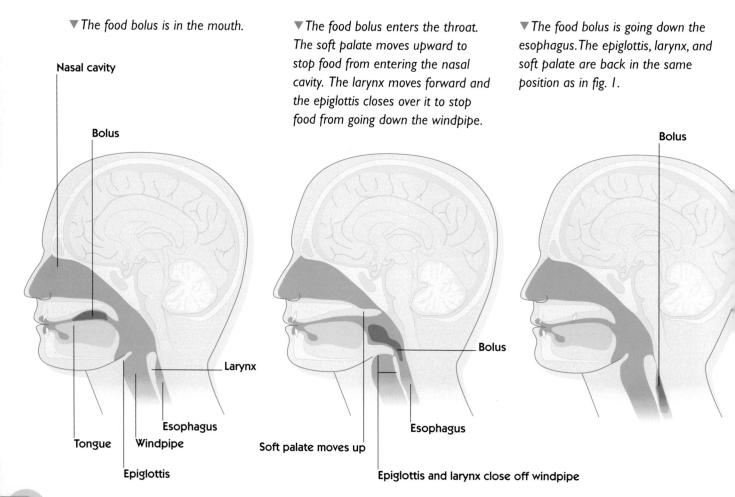

Nasal cavity

Bolus

Larynx

Tongue   Windpipe

Esophagus

Epiglottis

Bolus

Soft palate moves up

Esophagus

Epiglottis and larynx close off windpipe

Bolus

Closing off the airways

As the food is approaching the throat, several things happen. The soft palate moves upward to stop food from getting into the nasal cavity as the tongue pushes the food into the throat. Working together, the tongue pushes back and the muscles of the throat squeeze the food farther down.

The larynx (your "voice box") is squeezed shut and a flap of soft tissue at the back of the throat called the epiglottis closes off the windpipe. This ensures that no food or liquid can go down the windpipe and make us choke. It is actually impossible to breath and swallow at the same time, but this is not a problem since it only takes a second to swallow.

Investigate

Choking is what happens when someone's airways are blocked, preventing them from breathing. This can happen when a large piece of food is swallowed accidentally and gets stuck in the throat.

If the choking is not too serious and the person can still speak, vigorous coughing may help to dislodge the food. You should know what to do if the choking is more serious— you could save a life. The actions you need to take depend on whether the person choking is a baby or an adult. Find out what you should do.

On its way

The larynx is pulled forward and down as we swallow, making the opening of the esophagus bigger. Continuing pressure from the tongue and throat muscles push the food past the epiglottis and into the esophagus, or gullet. The food bolus is propelled through the esophagus by strong muscular contractions.

Biting, chewing, and swallowing are the first steps of our food's journey through the digestive system.

Moving along

The esophagus is not just a simple tube down which food falls on its way to the stomach. It forms the first section of the digestive system, or alimentary canal, that runs all the way through your body. On its journey through the digestive system, the food you have eaten will pass through the stomach and then through the small and large intestines.

Peristalsis

After food has been chewed and swallowed, the food bolus is propelled through the esophagus by strong muscular contractions. Usually, it takes around four to five seconds for the bolus to travel the length of the esophagus and enter the stomach. The alimentary canal is made of muscle and it pushes the food along with wavelike movements. This muscle action is called peristalsis.

The muscle making up the alimentary canal isn't the same type of muscle that moves your arms and legs. This muscle is not under conscious control, but is triggered by nerves in the canal that react to the presence of a food bolus. It is a type of muscle known as smooth muscle. The muscle in front of the bolus relaxes while at the same time the muscle behind it contracts, pushing the bolus along.

Sphincters

Where one part of the alimentary canal joins another, for example, where the esophagus joins the stomach, there is usually a one-way valve called a sphincter. The sphincter is a ring of muscle that opens to let food pass and then closes again. It is like a gate that only opens one way, ensuring that the food moves in just one direction. So, if you stand on your head,

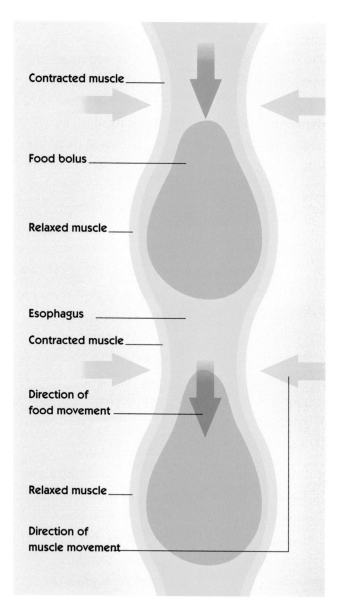

Contracted muscle

Food bolus

Relaxed muscle

Esophagus

Contracted muscle

Direction of food movement

Relaxed muscle

Direction of muscle movement

▲ *Food is moved through the digestive system by waves of muscle contractions called peristalsis.*

peristalsis will keep the food moving, and the sphincter at the entrance to the stomach will stop it from falling out again.

Lubrication

On the inner surface of the digestive tract there are a great many goblet cells. These are cells that are specialized to produce a mucus that coats the lining of the digestive system. This helps food to pass smoothly through the digestive system and protects the lining from damage by anything indigestible that has been swallowed accidentally.

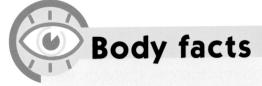

Body facts

Astronauts in low gravity conditions, such as low Earth orbit, have no problems swallowing. The muscular contractions of peristalsis don't need any assistance from gravity to move food through the digestive system. In fact, they are strong enough to work against gravity—the food will keep moving when you are lying down or even standing on your head!

Peristalsis keeps food moving along the digestive system—even in low gravity!

The stomach

Nothing further is done to digest the food on its short journey through the esophagus. The process of digestion begins again when the food reaches the stomach. Inside this muscular bag, the food will be churned with strong acids for several hours until it becomes a semifluid mush. At the same time, enzymes will begin to break down the large protein molecules.

As well as being the place where digestion really starts, the stomach also acts as a store for food. The stomach's storage capacity— about 3 pints (1.5 liters) in adults—allows us to eat large meals relatively quickly.

Stomach anatomy

The stomach is an expanded section of the alimentary canal, lying between the esophagus and the small intestine. It is shaped something like a fat letter j. The wall of the stomach is

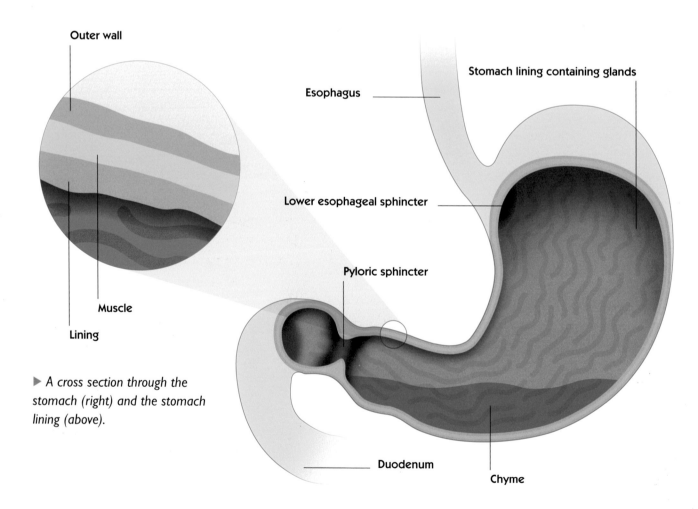

Outer wall

Muscle

Lining

Esophagus

Stomach lining containing glands

Lower esophageal sphincter

Pyloric sphincter

Duodenum

Chyme

▶ A cross section through the stomach (right) and the stomach lining (above).

muscled, like the rest of the alimentary canal. But the stomach has an extra layer of muscle at an angle to the first layer. This allows it to make the churning and grinding motions that break up the food, turning it into a semifluid called chyme.

The lining of the stomach has many small pits that are the openings of the gastric glands. Some of these glands produce hydrochloric acid. As well as helping to dissolve food, this acid also kills most of the harmful bacteria and other micro-organisms that might have been swallowed along with it. Other glands produce a mucus that protects the stomach lining from this acid.

Protein splitter

The stomach also produces a substance called pepsinogen. The acid in the stomach converts this into the protein-splitting enzyme pepsin. The pepsin gets to work on the proteins in the food, breaking them down into the smaller molecules of peptides and amino acids. An enzyme that splits proteins is called a protease (pronounced pro-tee-aze). The other main proteases work in the small intestine.

Leaving the stomach

After a few hours of processing in the stomach, the food is ready to pass on to the next stage of the alimentary canal. Very little is actually absorbed into the bloodstream through the walls of the stomach. That will take place on the next part of the journey along the alimentary canal. Another sphincter allows the nearly liquid food out of the stomach a little at a time and into the small intestine.

This is a picture of the lining of the stomach, showing gastric pits through which acids and enzymes enter the stomach.

Body facts

Have you ever wondered why your stomach sometimes grumbles noisily? After the stomach and the small intestines have been empty for a couple of hours, the muscles in the lower part of the stomach contract, beginning a wave of muscle contractions that move all along the length of the alimentary canal. These contractions clear out any remaining stomach contents, including mucus, foodstuffs, and bacteria. It is these muscle contractions that cause the rumbling noise we associate with hunger.

Digestive juices

Digestive glands in the body make the fluids that are needed for digestion. The salivary glands moisten food for swallowing and the glands of the stomach begin to break the food down. But the largest of the digestive glands are the pancreas and the liver.

The pancreas

Two things need to happen to the semifluid food, or chyme, that leaves the stomach. First, the acid that it contains has to be neutralized to avoid damage to the lining of the small intestine. Second, the process of breaking the food down that was started in the stomach has to be continued. The pancreas plays a big part in both of these processes.

The pancreas is located in the abdomen, and joins the first section of the small intestine.

It produces pancreatic juice, a liquid that enters the small intestine through a short tube called the pancreatic duct. Part of the pancreatic juice is made up of bicarbonate and water, which together make an alkali that reacts with the stomach acid and neutralizes it.

Pancreatic enzymes

The pancreatic juice also contains a number of enzymes that are necessary to break down proteins, fats, and carbohydrates. These enzymes won't work in acidic conditions.

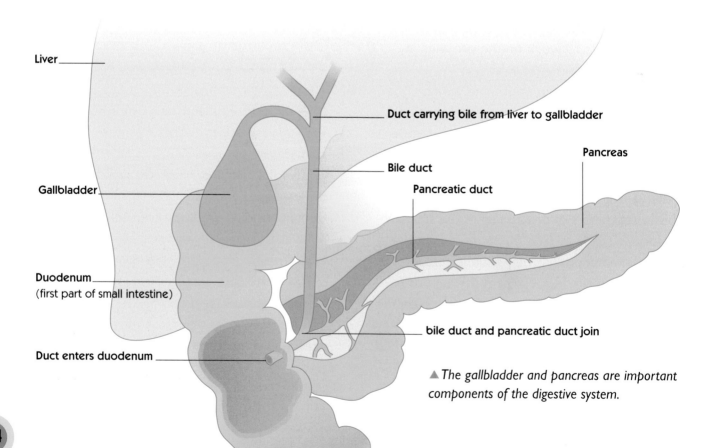

Liver

Duct carrying bile from liver to gallbladder

Pancreas

Bile duct

Gallbladder

Pancreatic duct

Duodenum
(first part of small intestine)

bile duct and pancreatic duct join

Duct enters duodenum

▲ The gallbladder and pancreas are important components of the digestive system.

Take a small bottle and pour some vegetable oil into it. Now pour a similar amount of water into the bottle as well. Put the lid on the bottle and shake it up. Then put the bottle down and watch what happens. The oil will soon separate from the water again. Now add a couple of drops of dishwashing liquid to the bottle and shake it again. What happens now?

Bile acts in a similar way to the dishwashing liquid. The dishwashing liquid separates the fat into tiny globules that become suspended in the water, forming a mixture called an emulsion.

As we see in this photograph, fats don't dissolve in water. In the digestive system, bile is needed to break them down into tiny globules.

Although the pepsin in the stomach began the job of breaking down proteins, most of this work is done by pancreatic enzymes such as trypsin and chymotrypsin. The pancreas also produces the enzyme amylase, which continues the break down of carbohydrate begun by the salivary amylase.

Fats also have to be broken down before they can be absorbed into the bloodstream. The pancreas produces an enzyme called lipase that will do this. But in order for the lipase to work effectively, another substance is needed as well. Bile salts also have to be present. These are produced by the liver and delivered through the bile duct into the first section of the small intestine.

Bile

Fats don't dissolve in water. In order that the pancreatic enzymes can get to work on them, the liver produces bile. This acts like a biological detergent that breaks up fats into tiny globules. These fat droplets are suspended in the watery pancreatic juices where the enzymes can break them down. Bile is stored in the gallbladder, a small, pear-shaped organ on the underside of the liver. Bile is released into the small intestine as needed.

The small intestine

The small intestine is a 20-foot (6-meter) long tube curled up inside your abdomen that receives food as it leaves the stomach. It takes an average of two hours for food to be pushed along the small intestine by peristalsis. As the food travels through, essential nutrients in the food are absorbed into the bloodstream.

Not so small

In spite of its name, the small intestine is not really that small. It is called "small" because it is an average of around 1 inch (2.5 cm) in diameter, and the large intestine is about three times that. The small intestine is divided into three parts—the duodenum, the jejunum, and the ileum.

The duodenum

The duodenum is only about 10 in. (25 cm) long, but this is where most of the digestion takes place. Digestive juices from the liver and pancreas enter the duodenum through the pancreatic duct and bile duct, and break down fats, protein, and carbohydrates. The absorption of vitamins and minerals into the bloodstream begins in the duodenum.

Into the bloodstream

By the time food has passed through the duodenum, it has been broken down into molecules that are small enough to pass into the bloodstream. The small intestine, particularly the ileum, is wrinkled inside and is lined with microscopic projections called villi.

Thousands of tiny hairlike structures called microvilli project from the surface of the cells that make up each villus. All of this enormously increases the surface area of the intestine.

▼ *A cross section through a villus, and a close-up showing the hairlike microvilli.*

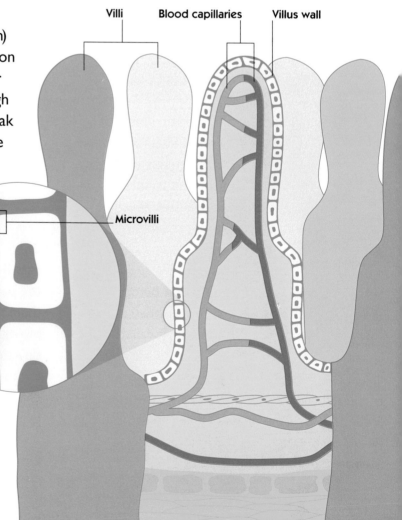

Villi   Blood capillaries   Villus wall

Microvilli

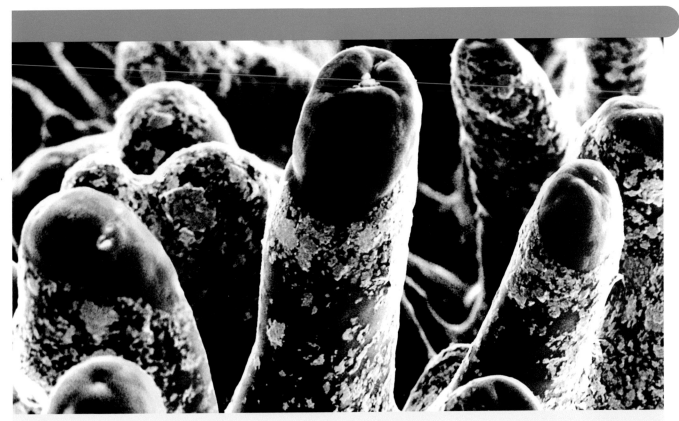

These fingerlike villi line the small intestine, greatly increasing its surface area.

Each villus has tiny blood vessels into which the digested food passes. Sugars and amino acids (the building blocks of proteins) pass across the cells lining the small intestine and are taken up into the bloodstream. These nutrients aren't sent directly to the cells of the body, however. First they will be transported to the liver for processing.

The small intestine is very efficient at what it does. Around 90 percent of the amino acid produced by protein breakdown and 95 percent of the fats will be absorbed during the food's two-hour trip through this part of the alimentary canal. What's left passes through another valve into the large intestine where it begins the final stage of its journey through the body.

Body facts

The inside of the small intestine covers an area that is five times bigger than that of your skin. It has been estimated that if it were smooth inside, it would need to be 2 miles (3.5 kilometers) long to have the same surface area.

The liver

The liver is the largest organ in the body, and one of the most important. The liver performs over 500 different tasks in the body, but here we will just look at a few of these tasks. It plays a central role in processing nutrients and maintaining the level of glucose in the blood. It also forms the waste product urea from unwanted proteins and breaks down harmful chemicals.

Unusual blood supply

The blood supply to the liver is different from that of any other organ. In the blood system, arteries carry oxygen-rich blood away from the heart to the organs of the body, and veins take deoxygenated blood back. The liver, however, only gets 25 percent of its blood supply from the hepatic artery. The main blood vessel entering the liver is the hepatic portal vein, which carries 75 percent of its blood supply.

▼ The liver is the body's chemical processing machine.

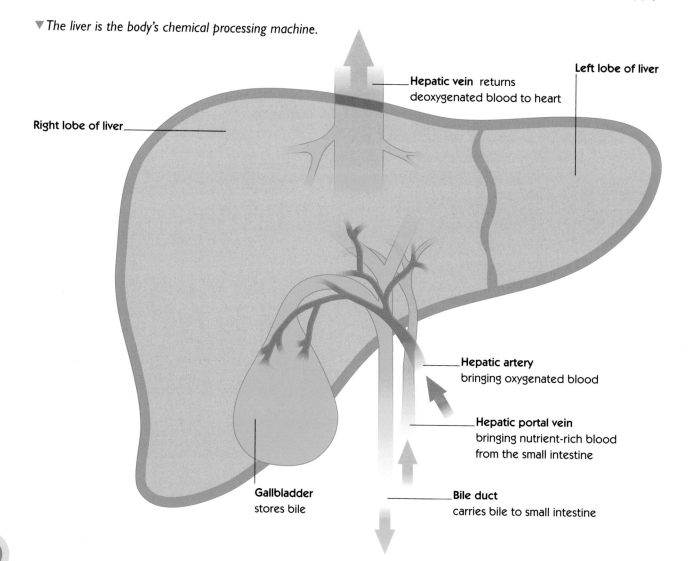

Right lobe of liver

Hepatic vein returns deoxygenated blood to heart

Left lobe of liver

Hepatic artery bringing oxygenated blood

Hepatic portal vein bringing nutrient-rich blood from the small intestine

Gallbladder stores bile

Bile duct carries bile to small intestine

Blood from the small intestine, pancreas, and spleen flows into the hepatic portal vein. Because of this, the liver is the first destination for the nutrients absorbed into the blood from the small intestine.

Blood sugar

The blood sugar level is a measure of the amount of glucose present in the blood. A healthy body will keep this level within fairly narrow limits. Maintaining the blood sugar level is one of the functions of the liver.

Glucose arriving at the liver from the small intestine is rapidly converted into glycogen for storage. When blood sugar levels drop in the body, the liver is triggered to begin the breakdown of the glycogen back into glucose. This is then released into the blood and transported to the rest of the body. If sugars are in short supply, the liver can actually begin to manufacture glucose from amino acids and other chemicals.

Fats and proteins

The liver is active in producing energy from the breakdown of fats. It is also mainly responsible for converting excess proteins and carbohydrates in the diet into fats. These can then be sent for storage in the fatty tissues of the body. The liver

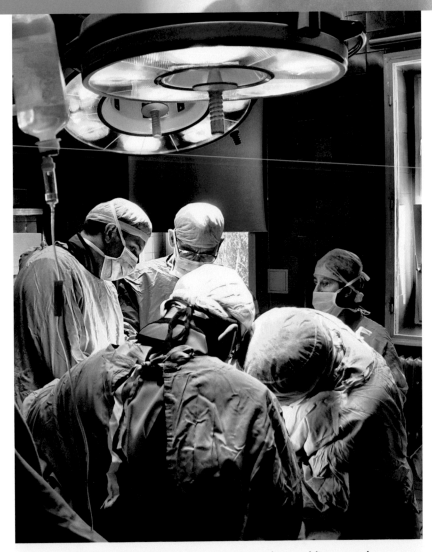

A functioning liver is essential for survival—a diseased liver may be replaced by transplantation.

assembles large molecules called lipoproteins that transport the fats through the bloodstream.

One of the waste products of digestion is ammonia, a highly toxic chemical that must be removed from the body quickly. It is produced when proteins are broken down and recycled. In the liver, ammonia is combined with carbon dioxide to form water and urea. The urea is filtered out of the blood by the kidneys and disposed of in the urine.

The large intestine

The large intestine turns around the small intestine in a loop about 6.5 feet (2 meters) long. The indigestible parts of food that weren't absorbed from the small intestine pass slowly through the large intestine, taking about 14 hours to go all the way through. Here, water and minerals are absorbed into the body.

The cecum

A valve separating the small intestine from the large intestine opens to let the remains of the food into the first part of the large intestine. This part is called the cecum. The chyme that passes into the large intestine is a watery liquid. Most of the nutrients have been absorbed by this stage, but the chyme will still contain undigested fiber as well as some minerals and vitamins. It is important to have fiber or roughage (indigestible parts of plants) in your diet. This is because fiber helps to move the food through the intestines and prevents problems such as constipation.

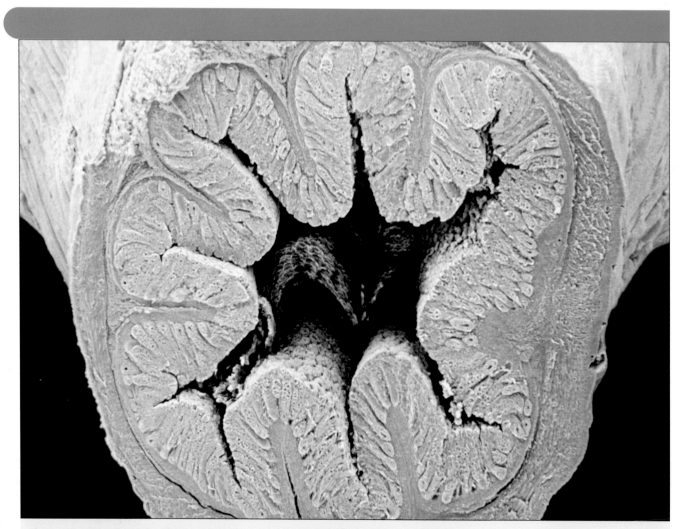

A cross section through a large intestine—you can see the folded lining and the muscle that surrounds it.

The appendix

Leading away from the cecum is a small tube called the appendix. The appendix leads nowhere and appears to have no function. Sometimes feces can become trapped in the appendix and the bacteria that live in the large intestine can cause the appendix to become inflamed. This results in the painful condition known as appendicitis. Generally, the only real cure is an operation to remove the appendix.

The colon

The colon is the longest part of the large intestine and can be divided into four parts. First is the ascending colon that follows on from the cecum and goes upward. The second part is the transverse colon, which crosses from right to left (transverse means "across"). Next is the descending colon, which goes down the left-hand side of the abdomen. The final part is the sigmoid colon, an S-shaped connection between the descending colon and the rectum.

As the chyme passes through the colon, it mixes with mucus produced by the intestine and with the large colonies of bacteria that live there. This mixture begins to form feces. As it moves through the colon, most of the water and some of the vitamins and minerals are absorbed through the lining of the colon.

The rectum

The feces are moved along the large intestine by peristalsis until they reach the rectum. This is the last point on the journey through the digestive system. Feces are stored here until they are ejected from the body through the anus.

Fiber from fruit and vegetables is an important part of a healthy diet.

The kidneys

Most people have two kidneys. These are located behind the liver and intestines, about midway up the back. Although they are not actually part of the digestive system, the kidneys play an important part in dealing with the waste products of digestion. They also keep the water content of the body in balance.

Water balance

Three-fifths of your body weight is water. The cells that make up your body's organs are largely made of water. Nutrients that the cells require are transported to them, dissolved in the water in the bloodstream. Maintaining the body's water balance is vital for good health and the organs responsible for this are the kidneys.

Cells generate energy by breaking down glucose, creating water and carbon dioxide in the process. All of this carbon dioxide needs to be disposed of. Some of it is breathed out; the rest combines with ammonia in the liver to form urea. Kidneys act as filters, removing urea from the blood. Excess water and urea together form urine, which is stored in the bladder until it is expelled from the body by urination.

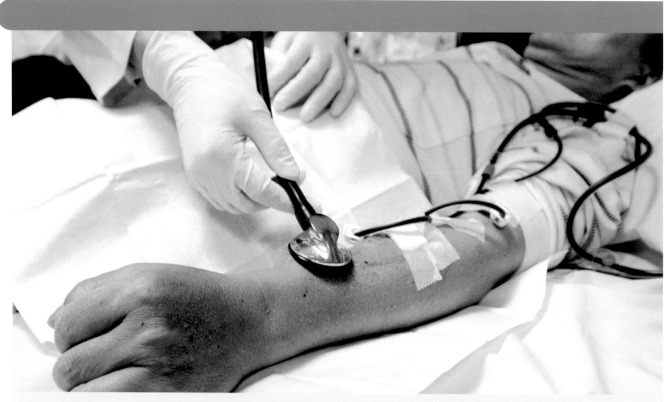

This person's kidneys are not working properly, so their job has to be done by a kidney dialysis machine.

Waste disposal

Each kidney is made up of a million or so nephrons. Nephrons are the kidney's filtering units. Each nephron has a tangle of blood vessels called the glomerulus, which sits inside a small pocket of tissue called Bowman's capsule. Water and wastes filter out through the glomerulus and into the capsule. From there, they flow along a tiny tube, or tubule, that extends from the Bowman's capsule.

Not everything passing through the kidneys is waste. A lot of it is chemicals that the body can still make use of. The kidneys ensure that chemicals such as glucose, sodium, phosphorus, and potassium are not lost. The blood vessel that formed the glomerulus winds around the tubule, reabsorbing the useful nutrients and most of the water. It leaves behind only the wastes that are carried to the bladder for disposal.

▼▶ *A cross section through a kidney (below) and (right) a simplified diagram of a nephron, showing how water and wastes filter out of the blood vessels and into the tubule.*

Body facts

Around 19 gallons (72 liters) of blood an hour flow through the kidneys. All of the blood in your body is filtered approximately every half an hour.

Every day, the kidneys process over 53 gallons (200 liters) of blood to remove about 4.25 pints (2 liters) of waste products and extra water.

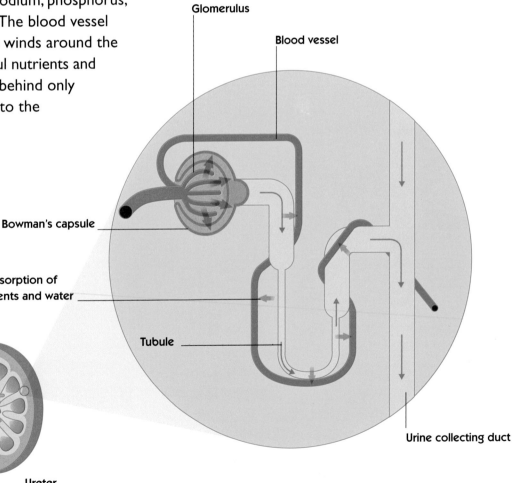

Glomerulus

Blood vessel

Bowman's capsule

Reabsorption of nutrients and water

Tubule

Urine collecting duct

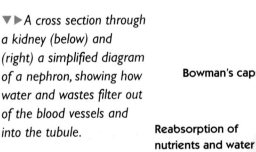

Renal vein
vein carries clean blood from the kidney

Renal artery
artery carries blood with wastes to the kidney

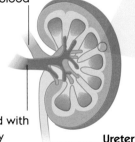

Ureter
carries urine out of the kidney

Bacteria and digestion

Your digestive system is home to billions upon billions of bacteria. There are actually more bacteria cells in your digestive tract than there are cells making up the human body. Most of them, sometimes called "friendly" bacteria, are useful to have around. They appear in babies soon after birth and are vital in the proper development of the immune system, the body's defenses against infection. Friendly bacteria also help us by digesting food that we can't digest ourselves.

Helpful bacteria

The large intestine does not produce any digestive enzymes of its own, but the bacteria that live there do. The large intestine has a huge population of bacteria that gets energy and nutrients from the remains of the food we eat. Some of the energy and nutrients are passed along to us and some are used to produce new bacteria that continue the good work. Other bacteria produce vitamins that are absorbed through the intestines.

Body facts

The total weight of bacteria living in the intestines of the average human is about 2 lbs. 3 oz. (1 kilogram). There are more bacteria in 0.035 oz. (1 gram) than there are people living on the Earth. It has been estimated that humans have roughly 10,000 million bacteria in their mouths, a billion bacteria on their skin, and a hundred billion in their digestive system.

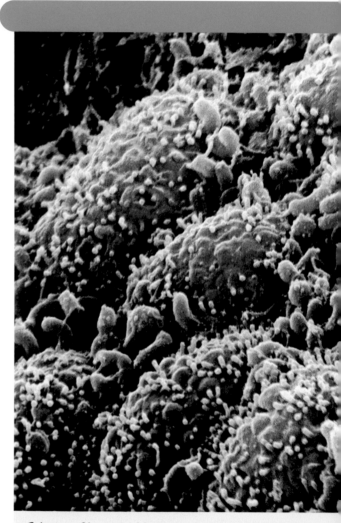

Colonies of bacteria (shown here in pink) live between the villi in the lining of the small intestine.

Fiber

The fiber in your diet is extremely important in keeping your colon healthy. Cellulose is a major part of plant fiber and a common part of a healthy diet. No animals can digest cellulose, not even herbivores such as rabbits and cows. However, there are many types of bacteria in the large intestine that can produce enzymes to digest cellulose.

Some of the products of cellulose digestion are hydrogen, carbon dioxide, and methane. They form intestinal gas, or flatulence. So, if you are ever embarrassed by an unexpected gas escape, you can blame your bacteria.

Antibiotics and probiotics

Antibiotics are used to fight off attacks by infectious bacteria, but they can often have the side effect of killing off the intestinal bacteria, too. This can affect our ability to digest food and cause ill health and digestive disorders such as diarrhea.

Some doctors now recommend that people use probiotics after taking antibiotics. Probiotics are dietary supplements that contain beneficial bacteria. They help to rebuild the numbers of bacteria in the intestine that the antibiotics have killed off.

Probiotics have also proved to be useful in the treatment of some diseases of the digestive system. One of the main uses of probiotics has been in the treatment of diarrhea in children, especially in diarrhea that is caused by a type of virus.

Probiotic yogurt may help to maintain healthy colonies of beneficial bacteria in the digestive system.

Everyday energy

The human body is a powerhouse of chemical reactions, in which many billions of molecules are built up and broken down every second. Some of these processes release energy but others need energy to make them happen. Together, these chemical activities make up the body's metabolism.

Metabolism

All of the chemical reactions going on in the body together make up its metabolism. It includes those reactions that take place in the digestive system where the food that we eat is broken down to release the nutrients it contains. Metabolism also includes those reactions that take place when the body uses these nutrients to release energy, to build and maintain cells, and to build energy stores.

Our bodies use energy all the time—but some things, such as cycling, need more energy than others!

By recording the number of steps you take in a day, a pedometer can help you to keep track of how active you are.

Metabolic rate

The amount of energy the body uses over a certain time is called the metabolic rate. The metabolic rate is not the same for everyone at all times. It depends on many things, such as age, body size, and how active we are.

To make a fair comparison between different people's metabolic rates, the rate is measured when the person is at rest, at a comfortable temperature and not hungry. This is called the basal metabolic rate, and basically, it is the energy the body uses while you're doing nothing except just staying alive.

Weight gain and loss

If we eat more than we need to keep our bodies functioning at a healthy level, we are likely to gain weight. If we don't eat enough, we will lose weight.

Eating a lot can actually increase your metabolic rate, as the digestive system uses up a lot of energy in digesting all the food. However, if you reach a point where the amount of food you are eating exceeds what you need for metabolism, then the body will simply store the excess, and you will put on weight.

If the body isn't given sufficient energy from the food that is available, it will need to use any stored fat. In extreme cases of malnutrition (lack of proper nutrition), the body will begin to break down muscles to provide the energy it needs. For good health, the energy intake from food and the metabolic rate need to be kept in balance.

Digestive disorders

If we eat healthily, then most of the time our digestive systems work well. But things can go wrong from time to time. For instance, constipation can be caused by a lack of fiber in the diet or by not drinking enough fluids. Diarrhea is often caused by an infection irritating the lining of the intestines. This results in feces being passed through too rapidly for water to be absorbed.

Food poisoning

Food poisoning occurs when someone eats food that has become contaminated by harmful bacteria. Often the effects can be fairly mild—the usual symptoms are vomiting, diarrhea, and pain in the abdominal area. Generally, healthy people will recover from food poisoning within a week or so. However, there are some forms of food poisoning that can be deadly and require medical treatment.

It is important to realize that contaminated food will not necessarily look, smell, or taste bad. This is why it is very important to maintain good standards of hygiene when handling and preparing food. You should store food properly and always wash your hands before doing any cooking. The cooking process and the acids in your stomach will kill many bacteria, but there is no point risking that something nasty might survive to do you harm.

Good hygiene is essential if you want to avoid an unpleasant experience of food poisoning.

Investigate

The bacterium that is most commonly the cause of food poisoning is Campylobacter. This is found in raw poultry, unpasteurized milk, red meat, and untreated water. The next most common type is Salmonella. This is found in unpasteurized milk, eggs and raw egg products, raw meat, and poultry.

See what you can find out about other bacteria that may be associated with foods and that may do us harm. What are the symptoms of infection caused by these bacteria? Find out what steps we can take to guard against infection.

Spicy foods such as chilies are loved by some people but can cause an upset stomach in others.

Vomiting

Vomiting is the body's way of ridding itself of harmful substances in the stomach or esophagus. However, it cannot get rid of anything that has reached the small intestine.

When vomiting occurs, peristalsis stops. This prevents the undesirable substance going any further along the digestive system. At the same time, muscles in the abdomen push the stomach up. They squeeze the stomach contents up through the sphincter that leads into the esophagus. Then the contents are forced out through the mouth. Our airways are closed off when we vomit, just as they are when we swallow. This ensures that vomit does not enter them and make us choke.

Staying healthy

The digestive system plays an important part in keeping the body healthy. By making sure you have a nutritious, balanced diet and by following the rules of food hygiene, you can help keep your digestive system and your whole body healthy.

Fun facts

The secret's in the teeth

Different animals have different diets, and they also have different teeth for dealing with these diets.

- Carnivores, such as cats and dogs, have ripping and slicing teeth called carnassials that allow them to kill and eat their prey.

- Grazing animals, for example, horses and cows, have big, flat teeth like grinding stones to break up tough grass.

- Insect eaters, such as many bats, have tiny, pointed teeth that are ideal for crushing hard insect exoskeletons.

- Seed-eating rodents, for example, rats and mice, have front teeth like sharp little chisels to crack the toughest nuts.

- Some animals, like the anteater, don't have teeth at all. The anteater uses its long tongue to scoop up ants and termites from their nests.

The teeth of a carnivore are shaped for killing and eating meat.

No spitting!

A human being makes more than 2.1 pints (1 liter) of saliva every day.

Space sauce

The first meal to be eaten in space was consumed by astronaut John Glenn on board *Friendship 7* in 1962. It consisted of pureed apple sauce squeezed from a tube.

A lifetime's food

The average male human will eat his way through 50 tons (45 tonnes) of food in a lifetime to maintain an average weight of around 154 pounds (70 kilograms).

A blue whale heads back beneath the waves after coming to the surface to breathe.

Huge appetite

An adult blue whale, the largest animal in the world, may eat as much as 4 tons (3.6 tonnes) of krill (a type of shrimp) every day.

Hydrochloric acid

The stomach produces about 4.2 pints (2 liters) of hydrochloric acid every day. Industry uses hydrochloric acid in refining ores, cleaning metals, removing scale from boilers, manufacturing fertilizers, and many other things. We prefer to use hydrochloric acid to digest our food.

It's peanut butter time!

In one year, the amount of peanut butter consumed by Americans is roughly enough to cover a sandwich the size of the Grand Canyon, or to fill enough jars to stretch around the world.

Hiccup, hiccup, hiccup...

Sometimes, if we eat too fast, eat something spicy, or gulp down a carbonated drink, we get hiccups. Hiccups are caused by the diaphragm, a sheet of muscle under the lungs. It suddenly squeezes and sucks air into the lungs, snapping shut a valve, called the glottis, above the larynx. It's the glottis snapping closed that makes the hiccup sound. Just exactly why the diaphragm behaves this way no one really knows—it doesn't appear to do anything useful.

The groom of the stool

This might not be the first job you'd think of applying for. The groom of the stool was responsible for wiping King Henry VIII's bottom after a bowel movement. This was a highly prized position, since the groom could spend time in private with the king.

Activities

Make your own yogurt

Milk turns sour when bacteria multiply in it. The bacteria's digestive processes produce lactic acid, and this turns the milk sour. By controlling this souring, we can turn milk into yogurt.

You will need:

- 1 pint (16 oz) of milk
- 2–3 tablespoons of plain yogurt (this provides your starter bacteria)
- A thermos
- A pan
- A thermometer (if possible)

1 Put the milk in the pan and bring it to simmer over low to medium heat. Be careful not to let it boil over.

2 Warm the thermos by filling it with hot water.

3 Allow the milk to cool a little. If you have a thermometer, check that its temperature has dropped to about 104°F (40°C), then stir in two tablespoons of yogurt. Pour the mixture into the warmed thermos (remembering to empty it of water first).

4 Leave the mixture in the thermos for about seven hours and allow the bacteria to get to work making lactic acid.

5 Pour the yogurt into a bowl and place this bowl inside a larger bowl full of cold water. This will cool the yogurt down quickly and stop the activity of the bacteria.

6 Cover the bowl with a plate or plastic wrap. Put it in the refrigerator to cool thoroughly.

After a couple of hours, you should be able to eat and enjoy your very own yogurt, complete with digestive system-friendly bacteria! Make sure that you follow these instructions carefully and before eating, please check with an adult that your yogurt is safe to eat.

Add some fruit to your yogurt for extra flavor—and fiber!

Color investigation

Food manufacturers use food colorings to make the things we eat brighter and more appealing. Colorings are controversial—some studies have linked certain color additives to behavioral problems in children such as hyperactivity. So, after you've done this experiment, perhaps you shouldn't feel too tempted to eat the remains…

You will need:
• Color-coated candies
• Coffee filter papers
• A saucer with a little salty water.

Open up the filter paper so that it will stand up by itself. Wet one of the candies and smear some of the color on the bottom of the filter paper. Repeat with different colors on different parts of the filter paper—don't put them too close together.

Now stand the filter paper—color-smeared part at the bottom—in the saucer of water. As the water is drawn up through the filter paper, you should start to see the colors separate. The red color should just stay as a streak of red. But how many colors are there in the green candy?

What you have done is a simple form of a technique called chromatography. Scientists use chromatography to separate the different constituents in mixtures and find out how much of each there is. Write down the results for each different-colored candy.

Bright-colored candies—appetizing or revolting?

43

Glossary

Amino acids often referred to as the "building blocks" of proteins, these small molecules link together in long chains to form large, complex protein molecules

Antibiotics substances obtained from various bacteria and fungi that are used to halt the growth of bacteria that cause disease

Bolus a mass of chewed food mixed with saliva that is swallowed

Carbohydrate one of the three main food groups, carbohydrates include starches and sugars and provide energy

Catalyst a substance that increases the rate of a chemical reaction without itself being changed by the reaction

Cell the smallest thing that may be classed as living; some living things, such as bacteria, are single-celled organisms, but others, such as humans, are multicelled organisms made up of trillions of cells working together

Cellulose a type of indigestible carbohydrate found in plant fiber

Chyme a thick liquid formed from a mixture of stomach juices and partly digested food

Enzyme a type of catalyst produced by living things; all enzymes are proteins

Esophagus a name for the gullet, the muscular tube that leads from the throat to the stomach

Exoskeleton the hard, protective structure on the outside of the bodies of many animals, such as insects

Feces waste material from the digestive system that forms in the large intestine and is ejected through the anus

Fat one of the three main food groups, fats include animal fats and vegetable oils, and are stored in the body as a source of energy

Fiber an indigestible food substance found in cereals, fruits, and vegetables that helps the intestines to function properly

Gland an organ making substances that are useful to the body, for instance, the pancreas is a gland that produces digestive enzymes

Glomerulus a cluster of tiny blood vessels that forms part of the kidney's filtration system

Impulse the electrical charge that travels along a nerve fiber

Metabolism the sum of all the chemical processes that take place within a living thing

Minerals simple chemicals that are needed by the body in small amounts to allow it to function properly

Nephron the filtering unit of the kidney; each kidney has about a million nephrons

Nutrients the substances, such as proteins and vitamins, that are needed in a balanced diet to ensure good health

Peristalsis the wavelike motion of muscles contracting and relaxing that pushes food through the digestive system

Pharynx another name for the throat, the space that leads from the back of the mouth to the esophagus

Protein one of the three main food groups; a group of complex molecules produced by living things to perform a variety of tasks in the body, including building cell structure and acting as enzymes

Saliva a mixture of water, salts, and proteins that moistens food in the mouth and begins the process of digestion

Sphincter a ringlike band of muscle that opens and closes passages from one part of the body to another

Taste buds groups of specialized cells found on the tongue that detect the different flavors in food

Urea a waste product formed from the breakdown of proteins; the body gets rid of it in urine

Villi tiny, fingerlike projections on the lining of the small intestine that increase the surface area available for absorbing nutrients

Vitamin one of a group of essential compounds that are involved in a variety of processes in the body and are needed in small amounts in the diet for good health

Further Information and Web Sites

Break It Down: The Digestive System by Steve Parker (Raintree, 2006)

The Stomach and Digestion by Carol Ballard (KidHaven Press, 2005)

What Happens When You Eat? by Jacqui Bailey (PowerKids Press, 2008)

Web Sites
Due to the changing nature of Internet links, Rosen Publishing has developed an online list of Web Sites related to the subject of this book. This site is regularly updated. Please use this link to access this list: http://www.rosenlinks.com/uhb/dige

Index